Homosexuality

State of Birth or
State of Mind?

Homosexuality

State of Birth or State of Mind?

by
Dr. Frederick K.C. Price

Harrison House
Tulsa, Oklahoma

Unless otherwise indicated,
all Scripture quotations are taken from the
King James Version of the Bible.

Homosexuality:
State of Birth or State of Mind?
lSBN 0-89274-574-6
Copyright © 1989 by Frederick K.C. Price
Crenshaw Christian Center
P. O. Box 90000
Los Angeles, California 90009

Published by **Harrison House, Inc.**
P. O. Box 35035
Tulsa, Oklahoma 74153

Contents

Introduction

Introduction

The dictionary defines homosexuality as "a condition of or characterized by sexual desire for those of the same sex as oneself."*

There is no doubt that this condition has existed since man began to multiply and replenish the earth. Consequently, many who subscribe to the dictates of this aberration believe that it is a state of birth and a natural part of human sexuality.

But what does the Bible say?

I believe that the Bible has an answer for everything that confronts us in the world. God, in His care and concern for mankind, has given us, through His Word, guidelines for living so that

---

Webster's New World Dictionary, 3rd College Ed., s.v. "homosexual."

we might live godly and peaceable lives in all honesty and integrity. If God is interested in our lives, then He is also interested in our sexual activity.

Therefore, we can look to God's Word, the Bible, with confidence for the answers and solutions to the complexities that face us every day, including the answer to the age-old question, *"Is homosexuality a state of birth, or a state of mind?"*

1
Proof That God Exists

Have you ever heard anyone say that the existence of God cannot be proved?

Well, if He does not exist, it really doesn't matter. But if by chance He does exist, then He would be the One to Whom the world would have to answer for not believing and acknowledging Him.

Now if God says His existence can be proved, and a person refuses to accept that proof, then that individual does not have any excuse. The existence of God can absolutely be proved — He says so in His Word, the Bible.

> For the *invisible things of him* (that is, God) **from the creation of the world are** *clearly seen....*
>
> **Romans 1:20**

When this verse says "from the creation," it does not mean from the day that the creation started all the way up through time until this point in history. That is not what it is talking about.

What it is talking about is the fact that the existence of the invisible God can be proved by the visible evidence of the physical world which actually exists in time and space.

> **For the invisible things of him (God) from the creation of the world are clearly seen,** *being understood by the things that are made....*

In other words, the existence of the world proves the existence of God.

> **For the invisible things of him from the creation of the world are clearly seen, being understood by the things that are made, even his eternal power and Godhead;** *so that they* **(those who deny the existence of God) are without excuse.**
>
> **Romans 1:20**

So this means that if you take the position of an atheist and claim that there is no God, then you do not have any excuse. When you stand before the judgment bar of God to give account to Him Whose grace and love you have spurned, Him Whose very existence you have denied, you are going to be cast into hell — the lake of fire. This is according to God, not Fred Price.

If you are an agnostic and say that you are not sure that there is a God, that He may exist, but that you do not believe He can be known personally, you are refusing both the evidence of your own senses and the eternal Word of God. In that case, the Bible says that you do not have any excuse, because God *can* be known — by the things that are seen in this physical world.

God Is the First Cause

There is a scientific premise that is absolutely irrefutable. It is called the principle of "cause and effect." It states that for every effect there is a cause.

This physical planet is an effect, because it is obvious that it could not have brought itself into being. Something, or Someone, had to cause it to exist. If it is an effect, a creation, then there has to be a cause, a creator. God is the cause. In fact, He is the first cause, the ultimate cause.

You Have No Excuse

If you say that the existence of God cannot be proved, just remember: you had better clean up your act and get your brief together before you go into God's court. When you appear before the Righteous Judge of the Universe with that kind of case, you are going to be thrown out, because He plainly states in His Word that you have no excuse. He declares that you *can* prove His existence — by recognizing the existence of the world which He created and brought into being.

2
Natural or Unnatural?

Because that, when they knew God, they glorified him not as God, neither were thankful; but became vain in their imagination, and their foolish heart was darkened.

Professing themselves to be wise, they became fools.

And changed the glory of the uncorruptible God into an image made like to corruptible man, and to birds, and fourfooted beasts, and creeping things.

Wherefore *God also gave them up to uncleanness through the lusts of their own hearts, to dishonour their own bodies between themselves;*

Who changed the truth of God into a lie, and worshipped and served the creature more than the Creator, who is blessed for ever. Amen.

Romans 1:21-25

This passage reveals to us the origin of homosexuality. According to the

Bible, homosexuality is the outward expression of the lusts of the heart of those who do not accept the existence of God, those who refuse to glorify or be thankful to Him, those who change the truth of God into a lie. Aberrant sexual behavior is the result of a denial of God and His Word of truth.

Natural and Unnatural Use

For this cause also God gave them up unto vile affections: for even their women did change the natural use into that which is *against nature*:

And likewise also the men, leaving the *natural use* of the woman, burned in their lust one toward another; men with men working that which is unseemly, and receiving in themselves that recompence of their error which was meet.

And even as they did not like to retain God in their knowledge, God gave them over to a reprobate mind (that, is a mind devoid of judgment), to do those things which are not convenient.

Romans 1:26-28

14

I would like to call your attention to the phrases "natural use" and "against nature." Now if there is a natural, there has to be a counterpart, which would be the unnatural.

The word *natural* implies that its opposite would be *unnatural*. Everything has a reciprocal. For north, there is south; for up, there is down; for male, there is female; for light, there is dark; and for hot, there is cold. Now if there is a natural use, there also has to be an unnatural use.

The Bible, not Fred Price, says that these people, both men and women, "changed the natural use into that which is against nature" — that is, into that which is unnatural.

What Is Natural?

In order to explain this concept of the natural and the unnatural, let me use an illustration which I call my "organ recital" premise. What do I mean by an organ? The eye is an organ, the nose is an organ, the heart is an

15

organ, and so is each of the parts of the physical body.

So how do we know what is natural and what is unnatural? Simple. All we have to do is look at our organ recital chart and discover the natural function of the different organs of the body. If we do that, then it should be very easy to figure out what the unnatural function of each organ would be.

Take, for example, the ear. What is natural for the human ear? To answer that question, let's take a look at what the ear can and cannot do.

The ear cannot see, or smell, walk or think. For it to do so would be unnatural.

There are two basic functions of the human ear. By looking at these functions we are able to discover its natural use. Obviously, the ear was designed to hear. It was also designed to house the balancing apparatus of the body. As we all know, balance is controlled in the deep recesses of the inner ear, which also serves the important outer function of hearing.

But let's forget about balance for right now and just deal with the fact that the ear was designed to hear and not to see, feel, smell, or taste. It is obvious then that the natural use of the human ear is for hearing. After all, if your ears are stopped up, you can't hear.

But just because ears were designed to be used to hear does not mean that they, like any other bodily organ, cannot be used for purposes other than their natural, designed use. Using an organ for a purpose other than its intended function is unnatural, although it is not necessarily wrong or improper.

Let me give you an example. I submit to you that your ears were not designed for earrings, yet you can wear earrings on them. Is that a natural or an unnatural use of the ears? It is unnatural. Is it a right or wrong, proper or improper, usage of them? That would depend upon the effect of the usage.

To my knowledge, I have never heard of any case history demonstrating that the wearing of earrings causes any kind of internal malfunction in either the hearing or the balancing apparatus.

So there is a natural and an unnatural use of the ears, but in this case the unnatural use does not impair the organ or interfere with its natural function. Nor does it usually cause a problem with the conscience, unless the wearer has some strong moral or religious convictions about wearing earrings.

The point is that a woman consciously deciding to wear earrings, although an unnatural usage of the ears, is not immoral or harmful to her body (unless she uses her adornment for immoral purposes or unless that adornment somehow hurts or injures her ears).

Nor does wearing earrings put most women into a state of depression causing them to have to visit a psychiatrist. It does not produce a real moral crisis or dilemma, requiring consultation with a pastor to determine whether the wearing of earrings is permissable Christian behavior.

So the natural use of the ear is obviously for hearing. It is absolutely verifiable that it is *not* the natural use of the ear to be adorned with an earring. That was obviously not God's original purpose in designing human ears. After all, to wear the type earrings that are most popular today, a woman has to have her ears pierced. If God had purposely designed the ear as a place from which to hang rings, He would have put holes through the lobes.

Now I do not think that there is anything physically, socially, morally or spiritually wrong with women wearing earrings, because I do not find anything in the Bible that indicates that Christians are not to do so. Nor do I see anything from a social, anatomical, psychological, psychiatric or medical standpoint that would indicate that the practice is in any way harmful or that it impairs the natural function of the organ.

Even though the wearing of earrings is an unnatural practice (since our ears were not designed for the sake of ornamentation), in the average human female this practice causes no problem with the body or the conscience.

But can homosexuality be considered natural, or even a harmless unnatural activity? I submit that the Bible makes it quite clear that it cannot.

3
Homosexuality Is
Against Nature

**...for even their women did change
the natural use....**

Romans 1:26

This verse describes lesbianism,
female homosexuality. Such sexual
activity is against nature.

Now if you are a lesbian, do not get
upset with me. I am not against you.
Just "be cool" and let me finish my pre-
sentation. I believe you will discover
that I am really trying to help you.

The Women Did the Changing

Notice that this verse tells us that
just as the men had given up "the natural use of the woman...in their lust one
toward another," so also "the women
did change the natural use."

Note who did the changing here.
This verse does not say that nature

changed her way. It does not say that God changed nature. It does not say that the environment changed it. It says that the women changed it!

Now I am not singling out women (we will get to male homosexuality a little later on in our discussion), nor am I coming against women in general. But there is a point I want to make here. I want you to notice something because I am getting ready to sweep away every so-called excuse, alibi and reason for unnatural sexual activity.

Notice verse 26 again, ...**for even their women did change the natural use**.... I want to emphasize the point that in this instance it was the women who did the changing of the natural order which God had established and intended.

No one can blame his homosexuality on the environment, on his parents, or even on the way he was born. The Bible clearly states that it is *people* who change their natural sexual drives in favor of unnatural ones. I want you to keep that point in mind.

The Change Was Against Nature

> ...for even their women did change the natural use *into that which is against nature.*
>
> **Romans 1:26**

This means that there are some things that are against nature. In other words, God has designed certain things to be as they are, as He intends them to be. People can violate and pervert God's design, but when they do, they are acting against nature. If something is against nature, it is against God, because God created nature.

Man for Woman, and Woman for Man

In our society today, there is a group of people who are called "lesbians." These are women who gravitate to other women for love and sex. The Bible says that this practice is against nature, that God did not make women for women, or men for men, but rather that

He made women for men, and men for women. To change that natural order is to go against nature and nature's God.

Homosexuality Is Not God's Will

> *And likewise also the men, leaving the natural use of the woman,* **burned in their lust one toward another; men with men working that which is unseemly, and receiving in themselves that recompence of their error which was meet.**
>
> **Romans 1:27**

There is a lot of discussion about homosexuality these days. In fact, it has come out of the closet and into the open, and is almost a commonly accepted way of life in many quarters.

With the various lobbyist groups promoting the homosexual cause, today situations and conditions that were formerly frowned upon have now become a part of our social lifestyle.

This is not the will and desire of God Who created the man and the woman for each other and for Himself.

Deal With the Truth

Jesus said, however, that ...**ye shall know the truth, and the truth shall make you free** (John 8:32). Therefore, we want to make sure that we deal with the truth.

The Bible tells us that is it unnatural for a woman to have any kind of desire for a sexual relationship with another woman. As we have said, such women are called "lesbians."

The other extreme is the group called "homosexuals" — men who desire sexual relationships with other men. The Bible says that both of these kinds of sexual activity are unnatural!

Some people get all upset when anyone brings out into the open the truth concerning this issue.

Some time ago I said something during one of my Bible studies about this unnaturalness while teaching on these verses of scripture. There was a young man present who was a homosexual. He wrote me a very lengthy letter, telling me that I was like all other bigoted ministers who were "down on" homosexuals.

I have news for that young man. I am not "down on" anybody, except the devil. I have nothing to gain by downing homosexuals and lesbians, but I do have a responsibility to share with them the truth of God's Word.

Homosexuality Can Be Helped!

Homosexuality (including lesbianism) is unnatural — *it is not ordained of God. It is not even biologically right or proper.*

People are homosexuals or lesbians because they will to be — *not because they can't help it!*

For too long, people have excused themselves by saying, "I can't help it."

For example, the young man said in his letter to me, "Well, you just don't understand; you don't have any real feeling for us. It's not fair; you should understand us and our lifestyle."

So I asked the Lord to help me understand. After all, I did not invent lesbianism and homosexuality. I did not put the expressions "natural" and "against nature" in the Bible; I discovered them in Romans 1:26,27 when I began to study the Word.

Then one day, as I was meditating on these verses, the spirit of God showed me something that I believe can help people involved in homosexuality — that is, if they want to be helped.

The "Bottom Line"

Now, there have been some who have said, "Well, I just can't help myself. You see, I was born this way."

That is a lie from the pit of hell! No one was born that way!

This truth is right there in the Word of God for anyone to see. I did not write it. In Romans 1:26 the Bible says that the women who engaged in lesbianism changed "the natural use for that which is against nature." In the following verse it says that "likewise the men, leaving the natural use of the woman, burned in their lust one toward another." It does not say that they, or anyone else, was born that way.

Homosexuality Is a Choice

Homosexuality is a choice that a person makes. An individual must choose to live as a lesbian or a homosexual.

In the following chapters, I will prove this point so that no cover will be left for the devil's lies on this vital subject.

4
A Biological Defect, or Unnatural Selection?

Let us say, for the sake of discussion, that you were born a homosexual. You have the physical atttributes of a normal heterosexual male, but the feelings and desires for those of your same sex.

You are a man, but you are drawn to other males and develop very strong feelings for them to the extent of wanting a sexual encounter with them. You were born with these tendencies.

You know it is not your fault. You had nothing to do with being the way you are. When you arrived on the scene of life, you had all these feelings within. In fact, you are unhappy when you are with women. Therefore, you only socialize with men.

You feel at ease with other males. You are repelled by females. You have tried to have friendly relationships with them (to go out on dates, to engage in boyfriend/girlfriend activities), but you have found that you are more comfortable with those of your own sex. You realize that you are a homosexual and you cannot help yourself.

Get the picture?

My wife is a female and she cannot help herself in that respect. She was born a female. But do you know that it was her choice and decision to get married? She did not *have* to marry.

On the other hand, I know of some women who have gone into a convent, become nuns and never married. They have all the female attributes that my wife has, all the same feminine desires, drives and attachments, but each of them made a volitional choice to become a nun, to dedicate her whole life to God — to never marry, have sexual intercourse, or give birth to children.

A woman who makes such a choice cannot say: "I couldn't help myself. I had to be a nun." No! She made that choice.

I know of men, normal in every way, who have had sexual intercourse with females. Then they had an encounter with God, became born again, and decided they were going to dedicate the rest of their lives to God and become priests. They made a vow that they would never marry, never have sexual relationships with a female, and never father children.

All these men had the same "standard equipment" — all the desires, all the feelings — of any other normal male, but yet they decided to remain celibate.

How did that happen? Can you say they could not help themselves, that they did not have any choice in the matter?

They Made a Choice

There may have been all kinds of pressures around these men to influence them not to enter the priesthood and live in celibacy, but they made their choices.

Are you following my analogy?

Could we say then that a man who made this decision could not help himself? That he had no choice but to become a priest? Not so. He made a choice of his own free will.

I know of other situations in which a man and a woman have come together, married and engaged in sexual intercourse regularly. Then both agreed not to have children. Both were still fertile. They could have produced children, if they had wanted, but they chose not to.

Could such people say that they could not help themselves? They have all the "standard equipment," all the normal sexual drives and desires, all the physical capabilities of childbearing, but they made a choice: "We are not going to have any children."

Well, if they remain childless, would you say that it was because they could not help themselves? No!

You Have a Choice

Then if you are a homosexual, don't tell me that you cannot help but love or desire another man. If you are a lesbian, don't tell me that you can't help being the way you are.

You can help yourself!

You do have a choice. Remember Romans 1:26,27:

> ...God gave them up unto vile affections: for even their women did change the natural use into that which is against nature:

> And likewise also the men, leaving the natural use of the woman, burned in their lust one toward another....

This passage tells us that women are made for men, and men are made for women, and not women for women and men for men. It also tells us that it was the women, and the men, who *made the choice* to lead an abnormal lifestyle.

Voices of Deception

There is no scientific or biological

evidence that a person is born a lesbian or a homosexual.

You were not born homosexual. You may listen to voices that come up out of the pit of hell and plant thoughts in your mind to make you *think* you were born that way and cannot change what you are, but that is not true — you have a choice.

I said it before: a woman makes a choice to become a nun and live as a celibate all of her life. She chooses not to get married, engage in sex, or have children. That is her choice. It cannot be said that her celibate lifestyle is just natural for her, because it is not. It is a choice that she has made.

The Choice Is Yours

You make a choice to worship God, or to deny God. You make a choice to be a heterosexual, or to become homosexual or lesbian. You make a choice to marry, or to remain single. You make a choice to become a Christian and serve God, or to become a murderer, liar, thief, whoremonger or alcoholic. You are not "born that way." It is all a choice you make!

The choice is yours!

5

We Are All Influenced

Now, I am the first to admit that we can be influenced by our surroundings and by other people. We are all bombarded with influences from the time we are children. When we do not even realize what is happening to us, we are continually exposed to influences of all kinds. But we don't have to yield to those influences.

We are all influenced, but it is still a matter of choice as to what we do about those influences. The man who is a whoremonger (a woman chaser) is that by choice. He was not born a whoremonger. He just lets his body govern and control him.

I could do that too. I have a choice as to what I do. I can say to my wife: "It's just natural for me to have other women. I'm a man, I have a man's thirst, a man's hunger. That doesn't mean I don't love you, Darling. I just have to have other women sexually because it's a natural part of being a man — I can't help myself!"

One time a woman came into my office and sat across the desk from me. When I asked her, "How may I help you?" she leaned forward in the chair, looked me in the eyes and said, "I want you, I need you, I have to have you."

Naturally, I could have made the excuse: "Well, I just can't help myself. It's just natural for me to give in to my male desires. Let's go lie down on the couch and do our thing."

That's right, we are all influenced, just as I was in that situation, but the question is: how do we handle that influence?

Are You Willing to Change?

Some people want to do right. They want to be helped, and they are willing to receive correction and do something about their condition. There are others who don't want to make any changes, so they do whatever comes naturally.

I will tell you what will come naturally — anything your mind can think of. Believe me, Satan will be there to feed you all the junk he knows you are willing to receive.

In that situation with the woman in my office, I could have done what comes naturally. I had a couch in there, and the doors were closed. I could have, under the guise of providing confidential office counseling, gone right to that couch with the woman and had sexual intercourse with her. She offered herself to me.

On another occasion, one of my assistants and I went to make a home visit at the request of a woman who regularly attended the church. Two of us went because I never go to a woman's home alone. I do not believe it is wise for any minister to make a home visit *alone* to a member of the opposite sex. It can be an open door to the enemy. (Eph. 4:27.)

At any rate, the lady had stated that she was having some problems and wanted to talk with a pastor about them. When we arrived at her house, she said to me, "I'd like to talk to you privately."

I said okay, and she and I went into the next room and sat down on the couch.

She looked at me and said, "I love you!"

"Praise the Lord," I replied, because that statement can be taken several ways. "You're supposed to love me, and I'm supposed to love you."

"Not like that," she responded. Then she said it again, "I love you."

"But I'm a married man," I answered.

Her reply to that was, "Are you always going to be married?"

Well, that was an offer. I know of ministers who have accepted offers like that. I could have too. I didn't, and I'm not going to. I just made a choice not to, that's all. (Prov. 7:21-27.)

The Devil Knows That Sin Is Pleasurable

In fact, I'll tell it like it is. God knows it, the devil knows it, and you may as well know it too. My body wanted to accept that woman's offer.

Now that natural bodily desire did not have anything to do with my love for my wife. My natural physical body would have liked to have given in to that temptation, but that is not what's important. It is what I did with that desire that makes the difference between sin and salvation.

Just because a thing gives pleasure does not make it right or ordained by God. (Prov. 9:17,18.)

When I look over my congregation and see some of those beautiful women, I could be tempted to kiss them. It could be pleasurable, but it would not be right. And just because I could get away with it without being caught would not make it right. I would be worse than Solomon with his 700 wives and 300 concubines.

The point I am trying to make is that neither God nor I will settle for that garbage about "I can't help myself; it's just natural for me to do that!" *That's not true!*

There is a choice to be made. Just as there was a choice which I had to make about having those two women. They offered themselves to me, but I made the choice not to offend God or to break my marriage vows.

My wife has been with me over 35 years. She can attest to the fact that I am all male from the top of my head to the soles of my feet. Absolutely! I could get into all kinds of situations if I would let myself, but I have made the decision that I am going to live the Christian life in truth.

Act Like a Christian

I do not deserve any credit for doing what is right, I am supposed to do it. I have been redeemed. I ought to act like a Christian, and so should you. I am trying to help people who want to be helped. Some people do not want to be helped, they want to live in the squalor of their immorality and sin. They want an excuse to do what "comes naturally."

They will try to excuse and exonerate themselves by saying: "Well, I *have* to do what I do, it is just natural, it's normal. You're just like all the rest of those preachers, you don't understand."

That is the biggest lie ever told.

I do not even have to talk about this issue of homosexuality and incur the wrath of some people, as I did with one young man when I first began to speak on this topic. He got up, disrupted the service, and walked out. It is an insult when people walk out on you while you are trying to help them. It is a slap in the face. I do not need to talk about this subject and run the risk of somebody reacting like that. I don't need that kind of grief. I don't appreciate it, and I don't have to have it.

I could just talk about issues that do not "rock the boat." Then everybody would say: "Praise the Lord, praise the Lord, hallelujah for Pastor Price. He's such a wonderful teacher." No wonder — he never says anything that amounts to anything! Because if you say anything that has any substance to it, you are going to end up hurting somebody's feelings or stepping on somebody's toes.

I will rock the boat!

Jesus said that the truth will make us free, and that is all I want to do, set people free by teaching them the Word of Life.

I can, if I want to, buy a purse. I have a choice, and I have the money. I can afford to buy one, but I do not use purses because purses are feminine. But I could say: "I can't help myself. I just have to have a purse."

That's garbage!

I could dress up, as some men do, in women's clothes. I could put on a wig,

makeup, false eyelashes and fake fin-
gernails, the whole bit.

But all of that is a satanic lie!

You Were Not Born That Way

If you believe that you have to
engage in homosexuality because it is
part of your inborn nature, that is Satan
feeding false thoughts to your mind.
You are not born with those desires, but
you can be that way if you choose, just
as I can carry a purse if I want to. I
know of no law that says I cannot own
and carry a purse. I can buy some nylon
stockings, some high-heeled shoes, and
a dress, if I choose to.

It is my choice if I use heroin. It is
not necessary for me to use heroin, but I
can if I want to. It is a choice whether
you like men or whether you like
women. It is a choice whether you
become a lesbian or a homosexual. That
is a choice you make.

You are not born that way!

If there is something in your past or
your personality that you cannot deal

with alone, you can come to the Lord
Jesus Christ, and by the power of God
through His Holy Spirit, you can be
changed and be the way you ought to
be.

6

God's Plan Is Procreation

The Bible tells us that women were made for men, and men were made for women. That is natural.

If anything else is natural, then God has jammed Himself into a corner. Because in approximately 150 years or less, the human race would become extinct. Two women cannot produce a baby, and two men cannot produce a baby. So if no more babies were born, eventually everybody on earth would die and the human race would disappear.

God Is No Fool!

The natural use of the man's body is not procreation — he cannot conceive or bear a child. He has no equipment for conception or childbirth. Men are not structured to have babies.

Now if God ordained homosexuality, then God would be a fool. But God is not a fool, He designed men and women to complement and fulfill each other in the role of procreation. That is the natural order of things.

Therefore, homosexuality cannot be natural, it has to be unnatural. It has to be against nature. Men and women are made differently, and their reproductive organs complement each other. Two male organ systems do not complement each other. Two men cannot produce a baby. The organ systems of two women do not complement each other, and cannot produce an offspring.

If homosexuality is natural, then two men ought to be able to produce a child, and two women ought to be able to produce a child. Anyone who cannot admit this fact is dishonest.

Only Women Have Babies

It is simply a matter of determining the natural use of an organ system. Women are the only human beings who are made to conceive babies, men are not. If man and woman do not get together, there will be no offspring, and the human race will become extinct.

So it could not possibly be natural for two men, or two women, to get married and live together. That is against nature, and if it is against nature, it is against God.

You may be one of those people who practice homosexuality and have never been caught. But deep down inside you know that it is not right. But because you have gotten away with it and judgment has not fallen upon you, you figure it must be all right. And because so many more people are doing it now than 10 or 15 years ago, that seems to make it right.

It's Still Not Right

Just because people are engaging in homosexuality does not make it right. It just means that society is becoming more degraded day by day. I do not speak to this issue because I have an axe to grind; it does not bother me if that is what you want to do. All I am trying to do is point out to you and alert you to the fact that homosexuality is against nature. And if it is against nature, then it is against God, and you are playing with fire.

Don't think you can get away with anything. The Bible says that there is a price you will have to pay. (Rom. 1:27.)

Apparently, from the beginning of time it has been natural for a man to have a woman in the context of marriage (I need to make this clear). So that means that God intended for men to marry women, and for women to marry men.

Adam and Eve, Not Adam and Steve

When God created the first man, Adam, and said that it was not good for him to be alone, He put him to sleep, took one of his ribs, and made a woman out of it. Then He brought her to the man. And Adam, because he had named all of the animals, also named the woman and called her Eve. (Gen. 2:18-25.)

He did not call her Steve. It is not Adam and Steve, but Adam and Eve. There are things that are unnatural. Sure, people can do them. Men are sleeping together, and women are sleeping together. But just because they do it does not make it right. And just because you can do it does not mean that it is right.

You can wear earrings, but that does not mean that your ears were designed for that purpose. You can wear all the gold on your ears that you want, but if your ears are plugged up, you will still not be able to hear. So wearing earrings does not make you hear. You hear because that is what your ears were designed to do.

There are other organ systems in the human body, and they have a purpose too. Just because you can do something else with them does not mean that that is their natural function.

> **For this cause God gave them up unto vile affections: for even their women did change the natural use into that which is against nature:**
>
> **And likewise also the men....**
> **Romans 1:26,27**

According to these verses, homosexuality is against nature. I did not write this passage, God did. Homosexuality is not new. It existed in the days of the Bible, and it has been going on ever since the devil has been loose in the earth. But it is not natural.

It is natural for a man to gravitate to a woman, and it is unnatural for a man to gravitate to a man. It is natural for a women to gravitate to a man, and unnatural for a woman to gravitate to a woman.

7

An Abomination to God

Thou shalt not lie with mankind, as with womankind: it is abomination.
Leviticus 18:22

In other words, God tells us that men are designed by Him to lie with women. He says that no man should lie with another man as he does with a woman. The Bible says — God says — it is an abomination.

We do not use the word *abomination* much these days, but the present-day English equivalent of abomination is the word *disgusting*.

God says that homosexuality is disgusting.

Neither shalt thou lie with any beast to defile thyself therewith: neither shall any woman stand before a beast to lie down thereto: it is confusion.

Leviticus 18:23

The Hebrew word translated *confusion* in this text means "unnatural." You can see that there is nothing new under the sun. Perversion did not start yesterday. It has been going on ever since Satan was loosed in the Garden of Eden.

Both the man and the woman committed that which is *unnatural.* In God's sight a man lying with a man, or a woman lying with a woman, or a man or woman lying with a beast — all are unnatural acts and disgusting to Him. (Lev. 20:15.)

Recently I read an article in a magazine which reported that a noted denomination had sanctioned and installed a homosexual pastor. Isn't that amazing? God said that such people ought to be stoned. (Lev. 20:15.) God said they ought to be put to death, and we ordain and encourage them to perpetuate the sin. What we should do is demand that they do exactly what we tell the alcoholic, the liar, the gossiper, the murderer, and the thief to do — *repent!*

Sin Is Sin!

The sin of homosexuality is just as much a sin as the sin of murder, lying, or stealing — there is no difference. Sin is sin, hell is hell, and the lake of fire is the lake of fire. The Bible does not say that the wages of committing a robbery sin, or a murder sin, or a lying sin is death.

The Bible says that the wages of sin is death. (Rom. 6:23.)

I don't care what kind of sin it is, sin is sin in the sight of God. Lesbianism and homosexuality are sins just like stealing, lying, murder, adultery, fornication or masturbation. If homosexuality was wrong under the Old Covenant, it cannot be right under the New Covenant.

Personally, I don't think any worse of the homosexual than I do of the adulterer, and apparently (from the study of the Bible) neither does God. He loves the sinner and wants him or her to repent and turn his or her life over to Jesus.

If a person truly wants to be free, *Jesus is the answer!* He said that the truth would set us free, and biblical truth still holds true today: *whosoever will, let him come!*

Dr. Frederick K.C. Price was born January 3, 1932, in Santa Monica, California. He attended McKinley Elementary School in Santa Monica, Foshay Junior High School, Manual Arts and Dorsey High Schools in Los Angeles and completed two years at Los Angeles City College. In 1976 he received an honory diploma from Rhema Bible Training Center and in 1982 was awarded an honorary Doctor of Divinity degree from Oral Roberts University; both institutions are located in Tulsa, Oklahoma.

In March 1953, Dr. Price married the former Betty Ruth Scott. They have four children: Angela Marie Evans, who is now Executive Vice-President of Crenshaw Christian Center; Cheryl Ann Crabbe; Stephanie Pauline; and Frederick Kenneth. Dr. and Mrs. Price have three grandchildren: Alan Michael and Adrian Marie, children of Angela and her husband Michael; and Nicole Denise, daughter of Cheryl and her husband, Allen.

Dr. Price has authored 14 books: *How Faith Works; The Holy Spirit — The Missing Ingredient; Is Healing for All?; How to Obtain Strong Faith; Faith, Foolishness or Presumption?; High Finance; Thank God for Everything?; How to Believe God for a Mate; Now Faith Is; Marriage and the Family; Concerning Them Which Are Asleep; Homosexuality: State of Birth or State of Mind?; Living in the Realm of the Spirit*, and *Origin of Satan.*

Additional copies of this book
are available from your local bookstore,
or by writing:

Harrison House
P.O. Box 35035
Tulsa, OK 74153